FRENCH
Learn the Easy Way

By Jacques Boucher

First Printing, 2012

Printed in the United States of America

Table of Contents

Introduction

Learning to speak French is not a daunting task. It should be a pleasurable effort and one that could bring you enormous rewards. Many people, when they return from a trip to France, will tell you that French people very seldom make any effort to understand you. Perhaps it is true that French people are a tad arrogant, but it is equally true that while in their country you should be able to pronounce their words correctly – it would help.

French is NOT a difficult language to learn. It was the language of many European courts until the fall of the Russian Tsars in 1917.

"Honi soit qui mal y pense" – King Edward III first introduced the phrase when "dancing with his first cousin and daughter-in-law, Joan of Kent. Her garter slipped down to her ankle, causing those around her to snigger at her humiliation. In an act of chivalry, Edward placed the garter around his own leg, saying "Honi soit qui mal y pense", and the phrase later became the motto of the Order of the Garter." The phrase is currently translated to: *"Spurned be the one who thinks badly of it."* To this day, the motto appears on the Royal Coat of Arms of the United Kingdom. This little bit of history is only to demonstrate to you that French has been spoken for many millennia and although it has endured many modifications and alterations, it has remained a very expressive language. One of the main reason for which French is an easy language to learn is because it is well organized. Each syllable is pronounced the same way in every word. There are practically no idioms in the language, nothing to remember, and nearly every word is constructed on the basis of its Latin roots. However, by no means do you need to know about the ancient language to learn French.

This book should help you construct words and phrases on your own, using English nouns that have the same roots in both languages. This book is dedicated to help you construct the French language from building blocks that I will provide for you. Moreover, I will endeavor to show you how the French body language is altogether similar and different from that of the Anglo Saxon attitude and manners.

The most fun you will have with learning French is perhaps when you speak to yourself. In fact, I recommend that you do so, on a regular basis. And I do mean talk to *yourself*. Getting used to the pronunciation of every word is one of the most important things that you can do when learning this language. Besides which, your brain needs to familiarize itself with the sounds of the French language. The best way to accomplish this is to listen or to watch television programs in French. Yes, it is a type of immersion, but one that you can do easily at home on your own time.

Therefore, this book will provide you with the guidelines and assistance that you will need to make your journey into the learning of the language a lot easier.

NOTE: Some of you may experience difficulties with the pronunciation of the French vowels, consonants and syllables. To help you in this process, we suggest going to www.forvo.com. This interactive site will assist you in learning to pronounce words correctly.

1. How long will it take to learn to speak French?

My first reaction to such a question would be to answer: "how long is a piece of string?" Everyone is different when it comes to learning a language and the circumstances vary from case to case or from person to person. For example, let's say that tomorrow, my boss sends me to France for three months; an assignment that will require me to have contact with French-speaking people on a daily basis. I am quite sure that when I return home, I would have learned a lot and would probably be handling a day-to-day conversation fairly well.

On the other hand, if, during this same assignment, my contact with French-speaking people was limited, I would certainly pick-up a few words here and there, but I wouldn't be able to handle a conversation at the end of the three months.

Most of the time a child will learn a language much faster than an adult will. And adults who are exposed to a variety of languages through their professional lives will also learn much faster.

Motivation also plays an enormous role into your ability to learn a language and into the length of time it would take you to learn to speak French. Say, your girlfriend (or boyfriend) is from France and you're intending to make a good impression on her (or his) parents. You will learn to handle a basic conversation in no time at all – believe me!

Your willingness to learn the language also defines the length of time it will take you to learn it. If you "must" take a course and really don't care one way or the other, then I am sure you won't be learning as fast as someone who is dedicated to speaking a new language.

There are three major steps to climb when you learn to speak French. The first is pronunciation of vowels, consonants, and syllables. The second is phrase construction in the present tense, and the third step is conjugation. This last step is perhaps the most difficult one to climb, but when you gain an understanding of how the verbs' conjugations work, you'll soon get the knack of it.

I repeat, French is easy to learn because it is an organized language. The building blocks of the language are consistent and you will find very little variance in the rules which allow you to construct the language with ease and speed.

Therefore, the suggestion that I would have for you, is not to set a time-line to learn French, but rather set a goal or a series of goals.

2. The Construction Blocks

The series of goals that are designed to allow you to learn the language faster are divided into three steps. The first of which is to learn the alphabet's pronunciation, vowels (with and without accents), consonants and syllables.

The Vowels and Accents

The vowels listed below with their pronunciations are phonetically simplified for easier learning. There are variance and exceptions but, at this point, we are not going to dwell on these.

The vowels are the same in English as they are in French, except that 'Y' is also considered as a vowel.

'a, e, i, o, u, y' are the six French vowels. They are pronounced the same way in every word, except for 'e' when surmounted of an *acute* accent as in 'prédire' or an accent *grave* as in 'après'.

'A' is always pronounced as when you open your mouth for the doctor and say '**Ah**'.

'E' without accent, is pronounced 'e' as in 'p**e**rceive'.

'É' will be pronounced as in 'd**e**dicate'.

'È' will be pronounced as in 'b**e**st'.

'I' has no exception: it will always be pronounced 'i' as in 'b**ea**k'.

'O' has no exception: it will always be pronounced 'o' as in 'h**o**me'.

'U' has no exception: it will always be pronounced 'u' as in 'd**ue**'.

'Y' has no exception: it will always be pronounced 'y' as in 'famil**y**'.

Where you might encounter some problems is when you see two vowels together such as in 'couloir' (corridor).

'OU' will always be pronounced as in 'y**ou**'.

'OI' is pronounced '**wa**' as in 'n**oir**'.

'EU' is pronounced 'E' as in 'p**ea**rl'.

'AI' as in 'J'aime' will be pronounced 'è' as if it were written 'J'**è**me'.

'AI' as in 'J'ai' will be pronounced as if written 'j'é' as in J**a**de.

'OE' as in N**o**el is pronounced '**N**ow**e**l' – simplified pronunciation.

'IO' as in 'permiss**io**n' is pronounced '**yo**n' as in '**yo**-yo' – very similar to the English pronunciation.

'IE' as in 'vie' is pronounced '**vi-e**'.

When you find three vowels together as in '**œu**f' (egg) – which is rare – you may pronounce it as if it were an '**e**' without any accent.

'OUI' is pronounced 'ou-y' or '**we**'.

Now, let's try this in front of the mirror:

Mature – Avoir – Dire

Permission – Oui – Faire

J'**ai u**ne p**o**mme – **Coeur – Devoir**

La nuit de Noël – J'aime – Vie

Beurre – Après – Doux

Découle – Domaine – Pupitre

There are other accents used over several other vowels; they are designed to enhance the sound of the vowel. For example:

Bient**ô**t (soon) is pronounced 'Bient**oh**'. Note: The 't' at the end of a word is generally silent – just ignore it!

Noël – although pronounced 'nowel' in most cases, the 'ë' is designed to enhance the separate pronunciation between 'o' and 'e'.

Most people who have attempted to learn French at one time or another will agree that some of the French consonants, or syllables comprised of vowels and consonants, are extremely difficult to pronounce.

Here is the list of consonants with their English pronunciation.

B = Bay

C = Say or Ka

D = Day

F = eff

G = jay or Gue

H = ash

J = gee

K = ka

L = ell

M = em

N = en

P = pay

Q = queue

R = air

S = ess

T = tai

V = vee

W = double vee

X = ix (as in six)

Z = zed

The Syllables

There is no *'accent on the wrong syllable'* in French. Every syllable is pronounced evenly. As for consonants, the written rule is simple – double the consonants if you wish to 'open the vowel' sound. For example: 'Sonnet' is the same in English as it is in French – it means the same thing and it is pronounced exactly the same way.

Here are some examples of syllable spreads:

Ab-do-mi-na-le – Abdominale – Abdominal

Ba-tte-rie – Batterie – Battery

Ca-da-vre – Cadavre – Cadaver

Dé-si-re – Désire – Desire

E-ten-dre – Étendre – Extend

Fra-ter-nel – Fraternel – Fraternal

Gra-ve – Grave – Grave (grave error)

Hu-meur – Humeur – Humour

In-vi-si-ble – Invisible – Invisible

Jus-ti-ce – Justice – Justice

Ki-os-que – Kiosque – Kiosk

La-men-ter – Lamenter – To lament (the death)

Ma-tu-ri-té – Maturité – Maturity

Nom-bre – Nombre – Number

Obs-cure – Obscure – Obscure

Par-don – Pardon – Pardon

Qua-tre – Quatre – Four (quarter)

Ran-ge – Range – Range (a range of)

Sa-ge – Sage – Sage (wise)

Ta-ble – Table – Table

Ur-gen-ce – Urgence – Urgency

Vi-ta-li-té – Vitalité – Vitality

Wa-gon – Wagon – Wagon

Xy-lo-pho-ne – Xylophone – Xylophone

Yo-ghourt – Yoghourt – Yoghurt

Zè-bre – Zèbre – Zebra

As you may have noticed, the words I have chosen above, all have similar meanings in French and English.

Remember: all syllables are pronounced evenly.

Below, I am introducing some of the more difficult syllables to pronounce. Such as a singer 'listens' to the 'sound' of his voice when recording a song, you need to listen to the sound of your voice when pronouncing the following syllables.

'**ON**' is perhaps the most common and most difficult. Just think of 'h**on**k' as in 'h**on**ky dory'.

The 'n' is silent.

'**AN**' is next. Again the 'n' is silent. 'An' is pronounced 'aun' as in '**aun**t'.

'**IN**' – In many instances the 'n' is audible which makes it very simple to pronounce – as in '**in**novation'.

'**IN**' for those of you who really struggle, I use sometimes the article "a" (as in a pen) and have them put a "p" or a "v" before the English "a". The result is oddly close to "pa**in**" (bread) and "**v**in" (wine).

'**EN**' is again pronounced the same way as 'AN' in '**aun**t'.

'**UN**' as in the number 'one' is strictly a nasal sound which is similar to '**un**'. Again, this is a difficult syllable to pronounce.

'**UNE**' is very easy to pronounce: '**u-ne**'.

'**CH**' is always pronounced '**she**'

'**PH**' is pronounced '**F**' – same as in English.

'**QU**' is always pronounced 'ka' as in '**qu**atrain'.

The easiest way to 'listen' to yourself is to wear ear-plugs and pronounce each of these syllables several times while only listening to the 'sound' you make. This is called 'internal voice auditing'. It is one of the most effective ways to learn the pronouncing of any language.

At first your voice will sound strange because you'll only hear the reverberation of your vocal chords, but that's what you want, since you need to master the sound they make.

Gradually, you will notice that repeating the same sound will help you in taming your voice and accent.

Practice makes perfect, and this is one instance where you need to practice until you 'sound' perfect.

3. Word Similarities

French is easier to learn than many other languages because French is an organized language, ruled by a set of grammatical and pronunciation guidelines. But let me explain. Once you've learned the rules – any of the language's rules – you can trust that it will not change mid-way through a sentence. There are very few idioms in French – as opposed to English, for example. The vocabulary is more restricted and therefore simpler to learn.

That brings me to the subject of similarities between languages. Many – thousands of words actually – are the same in English as they are in French. If you leaf through a French-English dictionary you will soon notice that many words are not only similar, but they are spelled and often pronounced the same way.

Here are 26 words that are similar between the two languages:

Accord – Accord.

Ballon – Balloon.

Carton – Carton.

Débat – Debate.

Education – Education.

Famille – Family.

Grand – Grand.

Hostile – Hostile.

Impression – Impression.

Jargon – Jargon.

Kidnapper – To kidnap.

Lampe – Lamp.

Marche – To March.

Nostalgie – Nostalgia.

Organique – Organic.

Passion – Passion

Qualité – Quality.

Réaction – Reaction.

Séculaire – Secular.

Terrasse – Terrace.

Uniforme – Uniform.

Version – Version.

Wagon – Wagon.

Xylophone – Xylophone.

Yacht – Yacht.

Zone – Zone.

And there are many more….

I suggest you try finding a dozen similar words for each of the letters of the alphabet (such as I did above), using a French-English dictionary. Once you have written them down – read each French word aloud, using the pronunciation you have learned in the previous chapter. (Forget about finding a dozen X, Y or Z words – there are not that many).

When you don't find a similar word for the noun you have chosen, try its synonym.

For example 'begin' has no similar word in French, but **commence** does – it's exactly the same in English as it is in French.

As a rule and since most English and French words have the same Latin root, synonymous words will mean the same in French as they do in English.

4. Gender

This is where the fun begins. In French everything has a gender. There is no 'neutral' in French.

In order to attribute the proper gender to a noun easily, think of what the noun signifies for you: Is it masculine or feminine?

Here are some examples:

Is a car masculine or feminine?

Voiture is feminine, of course. I can't imagine a car being masculine, could you?

Truck, on the other hand is much a male item. So, **camion** is masculine.

A machine is very much a female item. **Machine** is therefore a feminine noun. Notice the word similarity?

Each noun is preceded of a 'definite' (le, la, les) or an 'indefinite' (un, une, des) article which is simply designed to ascertain the gender (or number) of the noun. Nothing complicated about it.

Below are a few nouns with their articles:

La voiture ou une voiture – The car or a car.

Le camion ou un camion – The truck or a truck.

La lampe ou une lampe – The lamp or a lamp.

La table ou une table – The table or a table.

Le livre ou un livre – The book or a book.

As you can see, 'un' and 'le' are masculine articles, and 'une' and 'la' are feminine articles.

The only time these 'le' or 'la' articles change is when preceding a noun beginning with a vowel or an 'h', as in 'l'accord' (un accord is masculine, and the 'e' of 'le' has been replaced by an apostrophe). Or the word 'herbe' (herb) being feminine its article will read 'l'herbe' – the 'a' in 'la' was replaced by an apostrophe.

Now try to define the gender for the following words:

Armée

Bataille

Cave

Denture

Eléphant

Famille

Genre

Habitude

Innovation

Jardin

Kiosk

Lait

Manteau

Niche

Orange

Poison

Queue

Retraite

Sonnette

Tapis

Ustensiles

Vache

Wagon

Once again, I have chosen words that are similar in English and French. It should help you decide which is their gender.

Once you have found the gender of these nouns, verify your answers in your dictionary.

5. Singular versus plural

'S' is the secret! Truly, you don't have to worry about modifying a word when in plural – just add an 's' *et voilà* – you've got the plural of the word.

Again, let me give you some examples:

Une armoire – Des armoires.

Un bâton – Des bâtons.

Une chaise – Des Chaises.

Un diamant – Des diamants.

Un enfant – Des enfants.

Une fleur – Des fleurs.

Une galerie – Des galeries.

Une herbe – Des herbes.

Une idée – Des idées.

Un jardin – Des jardins.

Un kilo – Des kilos.

Un lavage – Des lavages.

Une mémoire – Des mémoires.

Une nation – Des nations.

Un ouvrage – Des ouvrages.

Un papier – Des papiers.

Un quartier – Des quartiers.

Un restaurant – Des restaurants.

Un site – Des sites.

Une tente – Des tentes.

Une urne – Des urnes.

Un vélo – Des vélos.

Un wagon – Des wagons.

I am sure you have noticed that all pronouns whether masculine or feminine have only one plural form: 'Des' or 'Les'.

The other letter that will indicate a plural is an 'X' which is put at the end of all the nouns ending with a 'U', such as in:

Bateau – Bateaux. (Boat – Boats)

Gâteau – Gâteaux. (Cake – Cakes)

Bureau – Bureaux. (Desk – Desks)

Given that all the nouns are either masculine or feminine, they will always be pluralized indeferently of their gender. Remember there is no 'neutral' word in French.

I have to apologize, but in the next segment I will complicate matters a little.

Although the gender of the pronouns and articles is related to the noun, the possessive pronouns are related to the possession (not to the possessor) – which is the opposite of the English grammar.

Let's take a girl and a boy – no doubt as to their gender.

And let's say the girl has a table: la fille a **une** table – **sa** table (Table is feminine.)

But she also has a cat: la fille a **un** chat – **son** chat. (Cat is masculine.)

The boy has a table: Le garçon a **une** table – **sa** table.

But he also has a dog: Le garçon a **un** chien – **son** chien. (Dog is masculine.)

When it comes to the first person (me) the possessive pronouns are used in the same fashion.

Ma table, **mon** chien.

However, the plural of the possessive pronouns does not change.

The boy has **some** dogs – le garçon a des chiens – **ses** chiens.

La fille a des tables – **ses** tables.

(*Me*) J'ai des tables et des chiens – **mes** tables et **mes** chiens.

6. Phrase construction and conjugation

In this chapter, we are going to use the construction blocks that we have gathered in the previous chapters.

To construct a sentence in French you only need to follow one rule: the words' succession rarely varies.

Article – noun – verb – adjective

The rose is red – *La rose est rouge*.

Or:

Article – 'qualificatif' (indicating quality) – noun – verb – adjective

The pretty dress is red – *La jolie robe est rouge*

Or

Article – noun – adverb – verb – adjective

The brilliant sun is hot – *Le soleil brillant est chaud*.

Or

Article – noun – verb – adverb

The sun is brilliant – *Le soleil est brillant.*

As you noticed, the article and noun always come first in most sentences. When you talk or write about something or someone, you put 'the subject' first then add the 'object'. The reverse does not happen in French.

A sentence is always constructed the same way: subject – verb – *and then the rest.*

We will now construct sentences using some of the words we have listed in the previous chapter.

We are only going to use the verbs 'être' (to be) and 'avoir' (to have) – in the present tense and in the third person.

Armée – L'armée est grande. *The army is big*

Bataille – La bataille est sanglante. *The battle is bloody.*

Cave – La cave est pleine. *The cave (basement) is full.*

Denture – Sa denture est blanche. *Her denture is white.*

Eléphant – L'éléphant est énorme. *The elephant is enormous.*

Famille – La famille est à la maison. *The family is at home.*

Genre – La fille a un beau genre. *The girl has a beautiful style.*

Habitude – Le garçon a l'habitude de parler. *The boy has the habit (or is used) to talk.*

Innovation – L'innovation technique est excellente. *The technical innovation is excellent.*

Jardin – Le jardin est très beau. *The garden is very beautiful.*

Kiosk – Le Kiosque est ouvert. *The kiosk is open.*

Lait – Le lait est froid. *The milk is cold.*

Manteau – Le manteau est vert. *The coat is green.*

Niche – Le chien a une niche. *The dog has a doghouse.*

Orange – L'orange est bonne. *The orange is good.*

Poison – Le poison est mortel. *The poison is lethal.*

Queue – Sa queue est longue. *His tail is long.*

Retraite – La femme prend sa retraite. *The woman is retiring (the woman is taking her retirement).*

Sonnette – La sonnette est bruyante. *The bell is noisy.*

Tapis – Le tapis est bleu. *The rug is blue.*

Ustensiles – Le chef a des ustensiles. *The chef has some utensils.*

Vache – La vache est blanche et noire. *The cow is white and black.*

Wagon – Le wagon est sur la route. *The wagon is on the road.*

Where the French language is different from English is when you rarely use an adjective before the subject.

For example, in English you say: the **red rose** is in the garden. In French it translates to: La **rose rouge** est dans le jardin.

Punctuation

Thus far we have not talked about punctuation. Punctuation, in French is as important as it is in English.

The French punctuation responds to the expression revealed by the sentence.

In effect, you punctuate a sentence as you hear it spoken. The rules are similar to those used in English but since the sentences are longer and more complex, the French punctuation matters as much, or more, than in English (comas everywhere).

For example – same as in English:

La fleur est rouge, bleue et orange –The flower is red, blue and orange.

Perhaps the most famous French author to have ignored – successfully – any form of punctuation is Marcel Proust. In many of his works, you would find pages after pages of beautiful writing – without any punctuation, except for a full stop at the end of a 26-page paragraph! I do not recommend that you follow his example and punctuate your written French text as you would in English.

Conjugation

Since this is not a grammar or a text book, I will not bore you with lengthy descriptions of the French conjugation. However, you will need to remember some easy rules to conjugate a verb.

In the present tense, most verbs are conjugated the same way.

Take the verb 'parler' (to speak) for example, it will conjugate as follows:

Je parl**e** – I speak.

Tu parl**es** – You speak (singular).

Il / elle parl**e** – He / she speaks.

Nous parl**ons** – We speak.

Vous parl**ez** – You speak (plural).

Ils / elles parl**ent** – They speak.

The end letter(s) or syllable is most often the same.

First person singular: – E (or S)

Second person singular: – S (silent)

Third person singular: – E

First person plural: – ONS (the 's' is silent)

Second person plural: – EZ (the 'z' is silent)

Third person plural: – ONT (the 't' is silent)

Unfortunately, these 'terminations' vary with each type of verbs.

Verbs are categorized by their 'infinitives'.

Verbs ending with ER (parler), RE (faire), OIR (devoir) and OIRE (boire) are conjugated somewhat differently. Nevertheless, the rules described above apply to most verbs conjugated in the present tense.

I would like to stress here that learning TO SPEAK French is quite different from learning TO WRITE French.

Therefore, I would urge you to concentrate on the pronunciation of the end-syllables of each conjugated verb rather than try remembering how to conjugate a verb in writing.

On the other hand, verbs are a necessary evil. For a start, I suggest you begin by using the most common verbs in the present tense. Everyone who speaks French fluently will understand you and will help you in case you make a mistake – because you give it a good try. Don't stay mute! The best way to learn to speak French for free is to speak it!

Here are some of the common verbs conjugated in the present tense:

FAIRE (to make or to do) – PERDRE (to lose) – ETRE (to be)

Je fais – Je perds – Je suis

Tu fais – Tu perds – Tu es

Il/elle fait – Il/elle perd – il/elle est

Nous faisons – Nous perdons – nous sommes

Vous faites – Vous perdez – Vous êtes

Ils/elles font – Ils/elles perdent – Ils/elles sont

DIRE (to say) – PREVOIR (to forecast) – AVOIR (to have)

Je dis – Je prévois – J'ai

Tu dis – Tu prévois – Tu as

Il/elle dit – Il/elle prévoit – Il/elle a

Nous disons – Nous prévoyons – Nous avons

Vous dites – Vous prévoyez – Vous avez

Ils/elles dissent – Ils/elles prévoient – ils elles ont

VOIR (to see) – ECOUTER (to hear)

Je vois – J'écoute

Tu vois – Tu écoutes

Il/elle voit – Il/elle écoute

Nous voyons – Nous écoutons

Vous voyez – Vous écoutez

Ils/elles voient – Ils/elles écoutent

Of the verbs listed above there are two that are used as auxiliary verbs: ETRE and AVOIR. Such as in English to be and to have play an important role in the conjugation of most verbs in **the past tenses.**

Let's use a frequently used verb (above) with its auxiliary.

J'**ai** fait

Tu **as** fait

Il/elle **a** fait

Nous **avons** fait

Vous **avez** fait

Ils/elles **ont** fait

It is important to remember that the verb stays neutral when using AVOIR as an auxiliary.

When it comes to using ETRE **in the past tenses**, the verb agrees with its auxiliary.

Je **suis descendu** (masculine) – Je **suis descendue** (feminine).

Tu **es descendu** – Tu **es descendue**.

Il **est descendu** – Elle **est descendue**.

Nous **sommes descendus** – Nous **sommes descendues**.

Vous **êtes descendus** – Vous **êtes descendues**.

Ils **sont descendus** – Elles **sont descendues**.

Let's try a sentence with each of these conjugated verbs.

FAIRE:

Je fais le ménage – I do (the) housework.

J'ai fait le ménage – I have done the housework.

La robe est faite – The dress is made.

ETRE:

Tu **es** dans la chambre – You **are** in the room.

DIRE:

Elle **dit** que – She **says** that.

Elle **a** dit que – She **has** said that.

AVOIR:

Nous **avons** des chiens – We **have** some dogs.

VOIR:

Vous **voyez** notre maison – You **see** our house.

Vous **avez vu** la maison – You **have seen** the house.

ECOUTER:

Ils **écoutent** de la musique – They **listen** to some music.

In the above sentences I have added some of the pronouns you will hear used very often. Try to incorporate these in other conjugated sentences of your choice, using the same verbs in different persons and using similar words to those you would use in English.

Write the sentences down on a piece of paper (or in a notebook) and repeat them aloud – in front of a mirror – and record your speech.

There is a very good website that will conjugate any verb for you.

http://conjugator.reverso.net/conjugation-french-verb-manger.html

I urge you to visit it but do not try to memorize any of it – as Einstein once said: *"I have a library, why would I need a memory?"*

You have a world library at your fingertips – you don't need a memory, just a tape recorder to listen to you speaking the words.

Don't forget to refer to the vowels and consonants' pronunciation you've learned already.

In French you also have a series of verbs that are called REFLEXIVE and RECIPROCAL.

The REFLEXIVE verbs emphasize the subject – the person who's speaking or the person of whom you speak. The RECIPROCAL verbs emphasize reciprocity – as in *'Nous nous aimons'* – we love *each other*.

Listed below are the reflexive and reciprocal verbs that you will find most often used in French.

Reflexive verbs

Se réveiller – to wake up.

Je me réveille à 7 heures du matin – I wake up at 7 o'clock in the morning.

S'asseoir – to sit (down).

Je m'assois sur le divan – I sit down on the sofa.

Se lever – to get up.

Je me lève à cinq heures du matin – I get up a 5:00 AM.

S'habiller – to get dressed.

Elle s'habille devant le miroir – She gets dressed in front of the mirror.

Se laver – to wash.

Il se lave dans la salle de bains – He washes himself in the bathroom.

S'appeler – to be called.

Il s'appelle Gilbert – His name is Gilbert or he's called Gilbert.

Se promener – to take a walk.

Je me promène dans le parc – I take a walk in the park.

S'arrêter – to stop.

Il s'arrête devant la porte – He stop in front of the door.

Se demander – to ask oneself.

Je me demande souvent – I ask myself often.

Se brosser – to brush.

Elle se brosse les* dents – She brushes her teeth.

Se dire – to say to oneself.

Je me dis que tout *va aller* mieux – I tell myself that everything *is going to be* better.

Se coucher – to go to bed.

Il se couche à dix heures du soir – He goes to bed at ten in the evening.

Se regarder – to look at oneself.

Elle se regarde dans le miroir – She looks at herself in the mirror.

*If you use a reflexive verb in a sentence where the subject is a part of the body, it will be preceded by a definite article (le, la, les) rather than a possessive article.

For example: Je me lave **les** cheveux – I wash **my** hair.

Reciprocal verbs

S'aimer – to love each other.

Ils s'aiment beaucoup – They love each other a lot.

Se détester – to hate each other.

Elles se détestent depuis l'enfance – They hate each other since childhood.

Se disputer – to argue.

Les voisins se disputent tous les jours – The neighbors argue every day.

S'embrasser – to kiss.

Ils s'embrassent en publique – They kiss in public.

Se parler – to talk to each other.

Ils se parlent au téléphone tout la journée – They talk on the phone all day long.

Se quitter – to leave each other.

Nous nous quitterons sans regret – We will leave each other without regret.

Se retrouver – to meet each other *again.*

Nous nous retrouvons *enfin* – We *finally* meet each other again.

Se téléphoner – to telephone each other.

On se téléphone tous les jours – We call each other every day.

Next on the list of difficult verbs are the Idiomatic Verbs. Unfortunately, like most idioms, the only way to use them is to memorize them.

Idiomatic verbs

S'amuser – to have fun (to amuse me).

Ils s'amusent dans le jardin – They have fun in the garden.

Se dépêcher – to hurry.

Elles se dépêchent pour arriver à l'heure – They hurry to arrive on time.

S'endormir – to fall asleep.

Je m'endors vers dix heures – I fall asleep around ten o'clock.

S'ennuyer – to be bored.

Je m'ennuie au travail – I am bored at work.

S'entendre – to get along.

Je m'entends bien avec mon frère – I get along with my brother.

Se fâcher – to get angry.

Je me fâche rarement – I rarely get angry.

Se marier – to get married.

Nous allons nous marier au printemps – We will get married in the spring.

Se passer – to happen, to occur.

Ces évènements se sont passés l'an dernier – These events happened last year.

Se reposer – to rest.

Je me repose dans l'après-midi – I rest in the afternoon.

Se sentir – to feel.

Il se sent bien maintenant – He feels good now.

Se souvenir – to remember, to recall.

Il se souvient de son enfance – He remembers his childhood.

Se taire – to be silent, to be quiet.

La petite fille se tait en classe – The little girl is quiet in class.

Se tromper – to make a mistake, to be in error.

Elles se trompent souvent – They are often in error.

Se trouver – to be (situated), to find oneself.

Je me trouve en face de la maison – I find myself in front of the house.

The next step is to tackle adverbs. Again, I'd like to use similar French and English adverbs and adjectives. The difference between using French and English adverbs or adjectives resides in their agreement with the subject of the sentence.

Here are some examples:

Le garçon est absen**t** – the boy is absent.

La fille est absent**e** – the girl is absent.

Le gâteau est **bon** – the cake is good.

La pâtisserie est bonn**e** – the pastry is good.

Le chien est courageu**x** – the dog is courageous

La femme est courageu**se** – the woman is courageous.

Le vent est for**t** – the wind is strong.

La brise est fort**e** – the breeze is strong.

Le technicien est exigen**t** – the technician is demanding

La mère est exige**ante** – the mother is demanding.

And now, you give it a try with the following adjectives and or adverbs:

Flottant, flottante, flottants, flottantes (adverb)

Grand, grande, grands, grandes (adjective)

Gentil, gentils, gentille, gentilles (adjective), gentiment (adverb meaning *kindly*)

Habitant, habitants, habitante, habitantes (noun or adverb. Verb: 'habiter')

Humble, humbles, humblement (adverb)

Irritant, irritants, irritante, irritantes

Joyeux, joyeuse, joyeuses

Lamentable, lamentables

Misérable, misérable (noun), misérablement (adverb)

Naturel, naturelle (adjective), naturellement (adverb)

Obéissant, obéissants, obéissante, obéissantes (*obedient*)

Pauvre, pauvres, pauvrement (adverb)

Quasiment (adverb meaning *almost* as in '*quasi*')

Rare, rares (adjective), rarement (adverb)

Sage, sages (adjective), sagement (adverb meaning *quietly* or *gently*)

Tendre, tendres (adjective), tendrement (adverb)

Utile, utiles, utilement (adjective/adverb meaning *useful*)

Valable, valables, valablement (adjective/adverb meaning *valid, validly*)

7. Idiomatic questions, phrases and using a dictionary

There are a few idiomatic questions that will be used constantly. They are not simple to remember or pronounce, but since practice makes perfect, try and try again until you succeed.

Qu'est-ce qu'il y a? – What is it?

Qu'est-ce que c'est ça? – What is that?

Qu'est-ce que tu veux? – What is it you want?

The prefix idiom remains the same for each of the question.

If you do not wish to use the prefix, you can ask:

Qu'y a-t-il? – What is it?

Qu'est-ce? Qu'est-ce que c'est ça? – What is that?

Que veux-tu? – What do you want?

The French 'Five Questions' are:

Quand? – When?

Où? – Where?

Quoi? – What?

Qui? – Who?

Pourquoi? – Why?

The answers to each of these vary, but generally are:

Quand – Hier (yesterday), aujourd'hui (today), demain (tomorrow), dans un jour (in a day), dans deux mois (in two months), etc.

Or more evasively: Pendant la semaine (during the week), dans la journée (during the day), de temps en temps (from time to time).

Où – Chez moi (at my place), chez nous (at our place), à l'église (at church), à l'école (at school), etc.

Or when you don't know the place, you could respond with: Quelque part (somewhere), ailleurs (elsewhere), nulle part (nowhere).

Quoi – Ceci (this), cela (that), ces (these and those).

Qui – Lui (him), elle (her or she), il (he), ils (they), elles (they).

Pourquoi – The answer to this question is generally a sentence preceded by the idiom 'parce que' (because).

Idiomatic French Phrases

You will probably hear these phrases spoken often when you are in company of French-speaking people or when you watch a movie. I suggest you repeat them as often as possible to familiarize your mind with them.

Nous voici – There we are.

Et voilà – There you are... Or there you go.

Je vous écoute – I'm listening.

Tu as du culot – You've got some nerve!

Au cas où – In case of, or in case that.

À votre santé! – Cheers! (To your health)

À mon avis – In my opinion.

À peine – Hardly, merely.

À tes souhaits – Bless you.

Ah bon (?) – Oh really?

Au fait – While I think of it, by the way.

Au fur et à mesure, petit à petit – Little by little.

Au lieu de – Instead of, rather than.

Avoir l'air (de) – To look (like).

Non, mais tu blagues! – No, but you're joking!

Comment allez-vous? – How are you? (Formal)

Comment vas-tu? – How are you? (Familiar)

Ça va, merci, et vous? – It's okay, thank you..., and you? (Formal)

Je vais bien, merci, et toi? – I'm fine, thank you..., and you? (Familiar)

C'est-à-dire – I mean, that is to say.

A vrai dire – To tell you the truth.

Vraiment? – Really?

Je n'en crois pas un mot! – I don't believe a word of it!

C'est parti – Here we go, and we're off!

Ce n'est pas vrai! – That is not true!

Ce n'est pas terrible – It's not terrible.

Jeter un coup d'œil – Take a quick look. To throw a glance.

D'ailleurs – What's more, moreover, in fact.

Du jour au lendemain – Overnight, from one day to the next.

En effet – Indeed, that's right.

En fait – In fact.

Être en train de faire – To be in the middle of doing something.

Faire le pont – To make it a long weekend.

Fais gaffe, faire attention – Watch out, be careful!

Fais voir – Let me see.

Figure-toi – You know what. Guess what/who?

Je pense qu'il faut – I think it's necessary.

Il m'en fait voir de toutes les couleurs – He drives me crazy!

Il y a quelque chose qui cloche – There's something wrong.

Je n'en reviens pas – I can't believe it.

Je n'y suis pour rien – I've got nothing to do with this.

J'ai du boulot – I've got work to do.

J'ai du pain sur la planche – I've got a lot of work waiting for me.

Il me raconte du n'importe quoi – He tells me anything.

Oh mon dieu! – Oh my God!

Est-ce qu'on peut se tutoyer? – Can we let go of the formalities?

Rien n'a changé – Nothing's changed.

Quand même! – Really, finally!

Revenons à nos moutons – Let's get back to the subject at hand.

Rien à voir avec ça – Nothing to do with this.

Si ce n'est pas indiscret – If it's not too personal.

Si tu veux – If you like. (Familiar)

Si vous voulez – If you like. (Formal)

Tout à fait – Absolutely, exactly, entirely.

On se voit tout à l'heure – We'll see you later.

Tout de suite – Immediately, as soon as possible.

Tu sais comment ça marche – You know how it goes.

Tu m'étonnes – Tell me something I don't know.

Non mais tu te rends compte? – Really, can you imagine?

Ça, ça vaut le coup – That's worth a try

.

In the past very few dictionary went any further than giving you the translation of the word. These days, most dictionaries are filled with conjugation, synonyms, and word-usage pages, which is exactly the dictionary you want.

Given the fact that you basically 'transfer' your English speech into a French speech, all you need doing in the first instance is to concentrate on finding similar words with similar meaning and usage. Then, you practice the pronunciation of these words and finally you put them in a sentence, using the present tense conjugation of whatever verb you choose.

There is no need to complicate your life with trying to learn the intricacies of the language – it would be a waste of time and effort. Remember, pronunciation is key to your learning the language. When you have mastered the art of pronouncing French words properly, you can advance to the next step, using logic.

In the realms of dictionaries, there is one that has always proven useful when learning a language – the 'word usage dictionary'. This type of dictionary, not only gives you the translated word, but its homonym, synonyms, pronunciation, and its usage in a phrase, expression, sentence and idioms.

This 'word reference' dictionary can be found on-line at

http://www.wordreference.com/fren/

Here is the excerpt for the word 'encore':

Encore:

Concise Oxford-Hachette French Dictionary © 2009 Oxford University Press:

<u>Encore</u>

When signifying 'toujours' **encore** is generally translated by 'still' and is used in an affirmative or interrogative phrase.

*Il était **encore** étudiant quand il s'est marié* – he was still a student when he got married;

*Habite-t-elle **encore** ici?* – Does she still live here?

Pas encore – Not yet:

*Elle n'était pas **encore** mariée quand elle a eu son premier bébé.*

She **wasn't yet** married when she had her first baby.

She **still wasn't** married when she had her first baby;

*Il n'est pas **encore** rentré.*

He hasn't come home **yet** *or* he **still** hasn't come home.

Some exceptions in the translations provided above and other meaning to the word **encore** are provided below:

ADVERB

1. (Toujours) still;

Je m'en souviens encore – I still remember;

Il n'est encore que midi – it's only midday;

Tu en es encore que là? – You have only reached that point?

Qu'il soit impoli passe, mais encore – the fact that he's rude is one thing, but still;

2. (Toujours pas) not yet;

Tu n'as encore rien vu – you haven't seen anything yet;

Cela ne s'est encore jamais vu/fait – it has never been seen/done before;

Les abricots ne sont pas encore mûrs – the apricots aren't ripe yet;

3. (De nouveau) again;

Les prix ont encore augmenté – prices have gone up again;

Encore toi! – You again!

Encore! – (À un spectacle) more!

Encore une fois – Once more.

Qu'est-ce que j'ai encore fait? – What have I done now?

Elle s'est encore achetée une nouvelle robe – She has bought herself yet another new dress;

4. (D'avantage) more;

J'en veux encore – I want some more;

Tu devrais encore raccourcir ta robe – you should take your dress up a little more;

Cela va encore aggraver les choses – it's going to make things even worse;

C'est encore mieux/moins – it's even better/less;

5.   (En plus)

Encore un gâteau? – Another cake?

Pendant encore trois jours – for another three days;

Il me reste encore 50 euros – I still have 50 Euros;

Que dois-je encore prendre? – What else shall I take?

Qu'est-ce qu'il te faut encore? – What else do you need ?

Et puis quoi encore? – What next?

Que dire encore? – What else can be said?

Ou encore – or else;

6.   (Toutefois)

Il ne suffit pas d'avoir de bonnes idées, encore faut-il savoir les exprimer.

It's not enough to have good ideas; one must be able to articulate them;

Encore faut-il qu'elle accepte – but she still has to accept;

Si encore il était généreux! – if he were at least generous!

7. (Seulement) only, just;

Il y a encore trois mois – just three months to go.

This type of word usage description really belongs to grammatical courses and formal French training, whether written or spoken. However, it is good to know that you can find out all there is to know about a word and its usage on the internet.

Another aspect of the word usage or word reference dictionary, which could be very helpful, is in the translation of idiomatic phrases.

For example; in English you say, "I've got the blues" – literally translated would read: "J'ai les bleus", which doesn't mean anything in French. This French idiom could be translated as "J'ai des ennuis" (I've got troubles) or "J'ai un sacré cafard" (I have a blessed cockroach!). As you can see, it's a two-way street when you try to translate anything literally.

The above remarks bring me to another difficult aspect of using a regular dictionary as opposed to a word reference dictionary: reverse translation.

Take for example the word: VIOLET – in French it translates to 'violet, violette' (adjective) the color or the flower.

However, in your word reference dictionary, you find:

Violet:

Concise Oxford-Hachette French Dictionary © 2009 Oxford University Press:

<u>Violet</u> / colors

I. noun

1. Bot violette *f*;

2. (color) violet *m.*

II. *Adjective* violet/-ette.

'**Violet**' found in these entries:

English:

Amethyst - purple - shrinking violet

Violet: Word Reference English-French Dictionary © 2011

Violet – (pourpre) – violet *nm.*

Violet – (rouge, bleu) – violet *nm.*

Violet – parme *adj.*

Violet – *Botanique* – violette *nf*

Violet: Word Reference English-French Dictionary © 2011

Compound Forms/Formes composes

African violet – violette africaine nf

Shrinking violet – personne timorée.

Violet-blue – bleu-violet, adj.

Violet-green – vert violet, adj.

Violet-purple – mauve violet, adj.

Violet-red – rouge-violet, adj.

When comparing the amount of information you receive in a word reference dictionary with that of a regular dictionary, you can immediately appreciate how useful the word reference dictionary can be.

LES COULEURS – *The colors*

Most colors are used in the same way, whether in French or in English.

Below are the colors often used in French:

Rouge – Red

Vert – Green

Bleu – Blue

Jaune – Yellow

Orange – Orange

Blanc – White

Noir – Black

Gris – Grey

Beige – Beige

Rose – Pink

For each of these colors you have a variation:

Rouge – Rougeâtre (somewhat red), pourpre (deep red), rouge cerise (cherry red).

Vert – Verdâtre (somewhat green).

Bleu – Bleuâtre, turquoise.

Jaune – Jaunâtre.

Go to your word reference dictionary and find the other colors as an exercise. Don't forget to read each of the colors aloud in front of your mirror.

8. How can I learn to speak French?

There are several ways to learn the language. You could take a course, spend months if not years in a classroom and become extremely proficient in French. Yet, when it comes to learn to 'speak' French, you are primarily endeavoring to train your brain to be receptive to French sounds and to the use of phrases and sentences on a day-to-day basis. This, of course, does not mean that you have to do away with French grammar altogether. It means that you are like a child learning the language of its parents. You are mimicking what you hear and joining words to action. You are learning to communicate – nothing more, nothing less.

The best and most effective way to speak French is to surround yourself with French atmosphere as often as possible. I don't mean fly to France every weekend or spend a month in a French-speaking country, no, I mean surround yourself with French books, French movies – either on TV or on the internet – and choose simple movies to start with. Without sounding biased, it is preferable for you to choose movies or TV programs from France or Belgium or Switzerland. Many of the other French-speaking countries have introduced dialectic forms of pronunciation, which could make it even more difficult for you to learn the language.

The main reason for surrounding yourself with a French atmosphere is to accustom your brain to the sounds and tonalities of the French language.

If you wish to learn to speak French, the principal ingredient in the mix should be your commitment to the task. Without flour, you might not be able to bake a cake; without commitment to learn to speak a language, you may never attain your goal.

Some individuals are gifted and will learn a language easily, yet most of us do not possess such a gift and have to work at it to attain the level of fluency that will allow us to be understood when speaking another language than our mother tongue.

However, 'working at it' does not mean that it has to be a chore. You need to have fun in order to enjoy the task.

9. I am learning to speak French

How can I learn French body language?

A cartoon would be most appropriate to describe French body language. Failing that, let's just describe a few of the most common gestures or body postures a French person will use or adopt when expressing their words in more descriptive manners.

Generally, a French person will 'talk with his or her hands'.

Practically every French adjective is accompanied by a gesture.

For example:

BIG will be accompanied by both arms extending upward and aside.

SMALL will be accompanied by thumb and index fingers hardly separated.

LONG will see a hand going from head to floor.

LARGE will see both arms extended outward.

Yet the most interesting and distinctive body language in French resides in the hands and feet's gestures. In fact, many of the hands' gestures do not need a word to be immediately understood.

Again, here are some examples:

A flick of the hand should dismiss the interlocutor from sight.

A pointing finger is a direct accusation.

A shake of the index finger indicates accusation, threat, or admonition.

A shrug of the shoulders (as in English), says, "Je m'en fou!" (I don't care).

Hands clapping, of course, indicate approval, or mocking what has been said.

As for feet or legs; watch carefully. The person speaking to you will quite often tap a part of his foot on the floor, indicating that he's heard enough or he's thoroughly bored with whatever you're trying to say.

And use less text books' elements of French?

Your body language is only designed to enhance what you're trying to say. It is not designed to use less text books' elements. The text books, whether you use them or not, only provide you with instructions, such as grammar and punctuation rules, but they rarely touch on the 'social' use of the language. And in order to apply the rules, you need to practice what you've learned either by yourself or during a formal course. 'Practice makes perfect' and nothing could be truer when learning a language.

Throwing away the text book is not going to help you – setting it aside will. Becoming familiar with pronunciation of syllables and consonants in particular, is one of the most important things you can do to learn French.

If you learned a thousand words, but cannot pronounce any of them correctly – you will have learned nothing!

And again; if you learned all the rules of grammar and even conjugation, but cannot pronounce the words of a sentence properly, you would have wasted your time!

Therefore, text books are to be used to learn the rules, but not 'how to use the rules'.

How can I learn to speak French without living in areas that speak French?

In this instance, we are talking about 'immersion' without being surrounded by French culture and speech.

I believe we have talked about this in previous chapters. The difference is that if you want to be immersed into a language without leaving home, you need to surround yourself with the culture and speech or find those things close to your place of residence. Yet, most often, the best case scenario is to sit in front of your TV screen and watch movies in French. If you have preceded these television-watching sessions with ample repetition of familiar words in French, you will be surprised of how much your brain has picked up already and how much you will understand of each of the shows you watch.

I hope you like 'action movies' because there are very few dialogues and lots of actions accompanying the words.

How can I learn French on my own?

If you mean 'learning French outside of a classroom setting', then there are three or four methods that will be useful for you to learn French on your own.

The first of these is to 'listen to yourself speak'. In fact, it would be preferable for you to be alone when you start talking to yourself!

The idea is to familiarize yourself with the tone of voice you will adopt every time you pronounce a French word or sentence. If you repeat the same French words as you read them, you will begin to articulate these words properly and without difficulty. And the next time you see the same or similar words written down, your mind will automatically adopt a French pronunciation for these words, phrases or sentences.

The next method, which could complement the first exceptionally well, is to surround yourself with French voices or movies on TV. Don't forget that your mind will store everything it hears and retrieve the data when you order it to do so. Text books and classroom courses will do the same. They are all designed to feed your mind as often and for as long as possible with French data. In my opinion, you do not need anyone to do that for you, you can do the same in the comfort of your own home – in front of the screen or mirror.

The third method, and perhaps my favorite, is to socialize in a French milieu. I don't necessarily mean go to France, but go to places French people frequent – French restaurant, cafés, clubs – and you'll soon make friends with French-speaking people who will love nothing better than to exercise your patience while learning the language.

There are many clubs or gatherings that you may be able to attend and which will offer you more access to the people and the language than you ever thought possible.

The first time you attend any such gatherings; you may feel uncomfortable or embarrassed. Don't be. It is better to feel embarrassed in front of a few friendly faces than in front of someone who's never met you. Moreover, these encounters will provide you with instant 'corrections' to your mistakes. Your French interlocutors will take no time to 'correct' your pronunciation and or add words to your vocabulary. And as time passes, your mind will react before you have time to 'think' about what you were about to say.

And this is the ultimate step in the learning process; when your mind becomes the 'boss' over your speech, then you know you are on the right track.

These are what I call reacting phrases or idioms that we use in English as we do in French.

For example:

Please and thank you.

Thank you and you're welcome.

How are you? I'm fine, thank you.

The same is true in French:

S'il vous plaît et merci.

Merci et de rien.

Comment allez-vous? Je vais bien, merci.

Once you start replying in French, you know you are on your way to learning French on your own.

With the assistance of the few pronunciation tips I have given you in the 'Little Grammar' section of this book, if you wish to learn French on your own, it would be a good idea for you to grab a dictionary and begin reading French words aloud in front of the mirror.

What is the difference between French in Canada and France?

Both languages have the same roots; however, they 'grew' differently.

In France, the language preserved its Latin origin and evolved slowly while monitored by the French Academy – an institution founded by the Cardinal de Richelieu in 1635 for 'The immortality of the French language.' The forty members of the academy constantly contribute to the policing of the language and to the adaptation and incorporation of foreign words into the language.

To this day, the French language spoken in France and in the majority of the French European communities abides by the rules and recommendations of the French Academy.

There are, of course, dozens, if not hundreds of dialects that have emerged separately over the centuries and within various regions of these communities. For example, in Belgium, one of the two official languages is Walloon, which is a dialect of French that has been spoken in the Ardennes (Southern Belgium) for hundreds of years.

Nevertheless, the language you will hear in Paris, Lyons, Geneva, Brussels, and other French city centers will be mostly based on the French Academic language.

Therefore, if you wish to speak French and use the language in most parts of the world where French is spoken, my recommendation would be to stick to learning 'French International'. This form of French is much like a passport to the French communities around the globe.

On the other hand, when you listen to a French Quebecois speak, even if you have spoken French all of your life, you may not understand what the person says.

There are several reasons for these differences.

In the first instance, French Quebecois has not enjoyed or followed the rules of the French Academy since the first French settlers landed in Quebec. The people and the language have been isolated for nearly four hundred years from their roots.

The second reason for the difference is the fact that the English influence has prevailed upon the language since the British infiltration and dominance over the province. Here again, the influence or insertion of British words into the language has mangled its roots to an extent that French people may not understand French Quebecois.

Here is a little anecdote to demonstrate my point. When we first landed in Canada in 1968, we had spoken French practically my whole life. After renting an apartment (with great difficulties, because of the language barrier), I ventured into one of the shopping centers with my wife – she wanted to buy a dress.

She went into the shop, chose a dress she liked and when she wanted to try it on, she asked the sales' clerk (in French), *"Auriez-vous ma taille dans ce modèle?"* – Would you have my size in this style?

The clerk looked at her uncomprehending. *"J'ai tout-sort de size, si c'est ça qu'tu veux* – I have all sorts of sizes, if that's what you want," she replied.

The clerk didn't understand what my wife asked because, primarily, she used the English word 'size' instead of the French word 'taille'.

Moreover, her answer should have read: "J'ai toutes sortes de **tailles** si c'est ça que **vous voulez**."

The second person 'tu' is a familiarity that is not polite to use when you don't know the person. And the sales' clerk didn't know my wife.

This sort of familiarity stems from the Anglo-Saxon culture whereby there is only 'you' for a singular or 'plural' address.

Lastly, if you compare the two answers phonetically, most of the Quebecois answer is composed of words enchained one onto the other. This 'eating' of words in a sentence, makes them practically impossible to understand either separately or together.

On another occasion, a neighbor of mine pointed out the window to a new car parked in the lot below the building saying, *"viens donc voir ce nouveau char!"* – Come and see this new car.

The word 'char' in French means 'tank' as in 'assault tank'. A car is translated to either 'voiture' or 'auto' (short for automobile).

Of course, I ran to the window wanting to see this 'new assault tank'. "That's not a *tank*," I said to her, "it's a car!"

"But that's what we call it in Quebec," he retorted, obviously annoyed that I would try to *impose* a French word to his Quebecois vocabulary.

For years – hundreds of years I should say – Quebeckers have resented the French for abandoning them to their fate in an inhospitable country (30 degrees below Celsius in the winter months is nothing to be grateful for) and have an almost innate dislike for their ancestry or antecedents.

In conclusion, although the difference between French Quebecois and French International is mainly phonetic, it would be very difficult for an English-speaking person to understand French Quebecois or even try speaking it.

How can I learn to speak French without attending any classes?

When you were just a child, did you attend classes to learn to speak? Of course you didn't. You learned the language of your parents by articulating your thoughts and expressing your desires or feelings.

French courses can and will only help you to learn how to write the language, the same as what schooling did when you went to elementary school. You already knew how to 'speak' your parents' language, the only thing left to do then was to learn the rules and apply them to your writing and eventually your speech.

What I am really saying is that you do not need French courses, classes or formal training to learn to speak the language.

As for 'How you would learn to speak French without attending classes', you need to follow some basic recommendations.

Your mind currently thinks in English. You react to the English language. You feel and sense all things in English. Your mind does not know how to recognize, acknowledge, feel or even react to French. Your mind is oblivious to the language because it has never been exposed to it.

Therefore, you need to 'expose' your brain exclusively to French. Generally, this system of learning is called French immersion. Many parents these days will send their offspring to language immersion schools, where the second language of choice is the only language spoken or taught within the school walls.

Of course, when it comes to an adult, a French immersion environment is not easily found. You may want to create such an environment by surrounding yourself with French culture and by mingling with French people in a club or association of sorts. Again, it is a matter of 'exposing' your brain to French sounds and environment.

When at home, try talking to yourself or instructing yourself to recognize your environment (in French) by naming all of the objects that surround you in French. Use your pocket dictionary to do so, and listen to the sound of your voice as you pronounce the words.

These are simple tasks, as simple as they were for you to learn to speak English when you were just a toddler.

Are there any quick and easy ways to learn French?

There are always quick ways or easy ways to learn something. However, what you really need is an 'effective' way to learn to speak French.

The quickest way to do anything is not necessarily the 'effective' way to do something – especially when it comes to training your brain. However, there are tricks that are very helpful and that will 'sink in' rapidly.

The first trick is to use idioms, such as questions (s'il vous plait) and answers (merci) as often as possible in your day to day lives. Even if people smile or find your behavior bizarre, don't bother – you're the one learning the language, not them.

The next trick is to turn on the television to a French program immediately as you get the remote control into your hands. Your brain is very much like a child – it expects to hear English sounds emanating from that screen, not French sounds. And as much as you want to understand the language spoken during that program, as much as your brain will want to record and familiarize itself with the strange sounds. Like a child, your brain wants to be able to react to these sounds when the time comes, therefore it will store the data away until, all of a sudden, you (or your brain) will blurt out the required words or even sentence. Someone will ask you something in French, and you'll surprise yourself by responding *in French*. That's when your subconscious has taken over and is digging into the data it has stored over the past weeks.

Same as a child will unexpectedly blurt out a word, a phrase, a sentence it has heard somewhere, you will too – as unexpectedly.

This is going beyond 'translating' words or trying to learn the language by rote, it is going from sound to brain and back. No translation required. And believe me it is a 'quick' and 'easy' way to learn to speak any language.

What's the quickest way to learn to speak French fluently?

Here again, I stumble on the word 'quick' when it should say 'effective'.

The reason I am so averse to the 'quick' mode of learning is because it's like putting on a Band-Aid over a gash that requires stitches. It would be a 'quick' fix, but not an effective or lasting solution.

Fluency is generally acquired over time, but you can speed the process effectively by listening to French people talk or record your voice on tape and play it back to yourself as many times as it would take for you to be satisfied with the results – that is hearing the same intonation in your voice, the same pronunciation of sentences or words as those you hear on television or radio.

This may not be as quick as you would like it to be, but it is certainly effective. Once again your brain needs to feed itself with the correct tone of voice.

Many parents have the habit of talking to their child in 'baby talk' as if their child was mentally challenged. If they continue to do this, the toddler's brain will not comprehend 'real', properly spoken words for an extended amount of time. Therefore, I suggest you don't 'baby talk' your brain into learning to speak French. Never, for a moment, think that your brain can't take it. In reality, it is forever famished of knowledge. Hungry for new input. So, give it what it wants and needs and you'll be surprised at what it can do.

How can I learn to speak French on my own?

If you are in a remote area – by that I mean that you don't have access to French-speaking people – then you need to create a French environment for yourself. You may either use the radio, television or internet to access a French-speaking community.

Once you have found a way to expose your brain to French sounds, you can then use all of the recommended systems or even tricks which I have described in the previous pages. Remember, you're not the one learning to speak French, your brain is. Same as someone who is learning 'touch-typing' whereby you can't look at your keyboard, when you learn to speak French, you don't 'look' at the words; you listen and register the sounds each word makes. Your brain will do the rest; it converts what it reads into hand motions or, in the case of learning to speak a language, it converts the sounds into meaningful words.

No translation required!

Can I learn how to speak French on the Internet? If so what are some good sites?

Yes, absolutely! There are quite a few sites worth visiting when you want to locate a 'training' program that will encourage your brain to register the sounds it hears.

My favorite site is http://www.jefrench.com/. The language is clearly spoken, the phrases are common and written at the bottom of each screen – or image. Therefore, it creates 'the environment' you require for your brain to listen and record the sounds it hears.

Notice that I used the term 'training' rather than 'courses', because, and once again, I will stress that you are 'training' your brain to speak French. You are not involving it into taking a French course. When the time comes to formalize what you have learned, then perhaps you will want to attend a French course. Yet, while you're still a toddler, there is no need or necessity for you to attend a course.

As for finding a software program that would help you learn to speak French, there are many – dozens of them – and the costs vary from $30 to $400. They're catalogued into various sections, such as 'home', 'business', 'trade', etc., depending on the circumstances or the communities you wish to tackle.

However, keep in mind that these programs are 'courses', which are no doubt helpful, and they will not be as effective as a 'training program' for your brain.

Besides, these 'courses' are not free, which brings me to the next question:

'Is there any way I can learn to speak French for free?'

If you wish to learn to speak French, there is no better way than doing it free of charge in your own time at your own pace and in the privacy of your home. Except for the times you want to mingle with French-speaking people in a casual and friendly environment, you do not need to pay anyone anything to learn to speak the language.

As I said, the best way to learn to speak French is to listen to the sounds, the pronunciation of the words and repeat what you hear as often as it takes you to attain practically the same sounds as a French person. When you go through these exercises of pronunciation, you might want to tape yourself and listen to what you said as often as it would take you to be satisfied with your repeated sounds.

Most of the websites dedicated to teaching French will encourage you to repeat what they say – until you hear and understand yourself as if you were a French person.

Of course, the French language, as any other language is not solely composed of nouns; it is comprised of pronouns, prepositions, adjectives, adverbs, 'glue words' and verbs.

What on earth are 'glue words' you ask? They are the words that hold a sentence together. Although different than those used in English, they have the same uses.

The glue words are:

Et – And

Ou – Or

à – At

Ceci – This

Ça (or que) – That

Ceux-ci or celles-ci – These

Ceux-là or celles-là – Those

Trop – Too

De or des – Of

Très – Very

Aussi – Also

Avec – With

Sans – Without

Pendant – While

Cependant – However

Jamais – Never

Toujours – Always

Souvent – Often

Rarement – Rarely

Chaque – Each

Entre – Between

Au dessus – Over, on top

En dessous – Under

A côté – Beside

A part – Apart

Pourtant – Although

Quant à – As for

Votre (or ton or ta) – Your

Notre (nos – plural) – Our

Encore, à nouveau, de nouveau – Again

Ne pas à faire – Not to do

Aucun, aucune – Neither

Jusqu'à – Until

Avant, devant – Before

Après – After

Arrière, derrière – Back, rear

Unfortunately, these glue words will need to be memorized at some point. There is no easy trick to using them except as in listening and recognizing them when spoken.

I'll give you some examples that you might hear often.

La fleur **et** l'arbre

Celle-ci ou celle-là ?

Je suis **à côté de** la table

Ton chien, **ta** chambre, **votre** maison

Notre maison, **nos** tables

Je suis rarement **à** la maison (I am rarely at home)

Le chapeau **de** mon père

If you were taking a 'course' in written English or English Grammar, you would be taught to recognize some of the 'glue words' possessive pronouns. However, since you are NOT taking a course, but only 'training' your brain to think in French, I recommend that you forget about the grammatical rules for now and only focus on memorizing and using the 'glue words'.

How can I learn to speak French fluently without living in an area that speaks French?

Living and working in a French city or country is, of course, one of the best ways to *accelerate* the learning process, because your brain is constantly exposed to the language – it has no choice but to learn to speak French.

Therefore, if you have no opportunity to be *immersed* in a French environment, you need to create a situation where your brain has no choice but to learn to speak the language! Remember, you are only a toddler – you have only your ears to listen and your mouth to speak. When it comes to learning a foreign language, your brain is about two to three years' old. It will fight you all the way, so it's up to you to expose it to as much of the language as possible – without respite. 'Eat, drink, sleep, and enjoy French' – that's the best and fastest way to learn to speak it.

In order to create such an environment, you only need three things: a television (with French programs or that can play DVDs), a computer where you can access a French website and a good French–English dictionary. The best French films that you could watch are often the classics, comedies, romances or even silent movies where the dialogue is written on the screen before (or after) each of the scenes is shown. Once you have watched such movies three or four times, you'll be able to recite and understand the dialogues without any difficulty. The trick is to accustom and adapt your brain to the circumstances portrayed in the film. And please, turn your mobile or cell-phone off during your immersion sessions. Your brain would like nothing better than chat in English while you're watching a French movie.

The next item on the list is your French learning website. This will be very similar to the work you would do with a child learning to speak. The teaching site shows you a scene with people interacting in various situations. The most commonly used are, of course, the tourist ones, such as meeting a French person, going to the restaurant and ordering a meal, checking into a hotel, etc. None of the scenes are complicated and are designed to have your brain register and store the French words and sentences it hears. Try to do this computer exercise as many times as possible – practice makes perfect!

The last item that you need is your dictionary. And here I must emphasize that you only want to use your dictionary when practice speaking or constructing sentences – not when you misunderstood a word. Put your dictionary away when you're watching a movie or work with the French website. The context of the movie scene should give you enough of a clue to understand every spoken word.

At first you will not be able to understand the entire movie, but don't despair, the more times you watch the same film the more you will understand it.

And I repeat: your brain will constantly look for an escape. You will feel bored, thirsty, or hungry; trying to think of something you miss doing during the day, or even feel sleepy. This is extremely common among people who begin *immersion* training. Any excuse will do – but think of how fast you could learn the language if you didn't succumb to all of these temptations. As I said, when learning a new language, you're like a toddler – constantly distracted – with an attention span of only 20 seconds! Once you have mastered the art of reclusive immersion, your attention span will grow exponentially. You'll become avid to know how the movie ends, what will be the next French encounter on your website and how many similar words there are between French and English – you'll even surprise yourself the day you realize that you've dreamt in French the previous night.

The next question I wanted to address is a little particular in the sense that it addresses only a very restricted segment of the population.

How can I learn to speak the French nasal sounds if I cannot hear or lip-read them?

Since listening and repeating sounds play a major part into learning to speak French, if you cannot 'hear' or 'lip-read' the French nasal sounds, you'll need to watch someone else speak both English and French sounds. For example the syllable 'ON' is part of, and pronounce the same way as the English syllable in the word 'HONK'. In addition, you should investigate what is called 'Cued Speech' (or FCS for French Cued Speech). This form of adaptive sign language enhances and improves the understanding of the differences that exist between French and English pronunciations. Here is a PDF-internet reference file which, I'm sure will help you.

http://www.cuedspeech.org/PDF/journals/vol6-4.pdf

Another way to learn to speak French, when you cannot hear or lip-read French consonants, is to watch a movie with subtitles. Without a doubt you will experience difficulties when trying to immerse yourself in the language, yet I urge you to persevere and even take a trip to Europe (Paris) if you can. Perhaps find an exchange program for the deaf that could house you in Paris, living with a deaf French family for a time.

A third method to learn to speak a language when you can't hear, is to plant yourself in front of a mirror and 'read' the French words (mouthing) them while using the pronunciation tips I have given you at the beginning of this book.

It will not be easy nor will it be quick, but, in the end it will be an effective way to train your brain to pronounce what it sees on paper properly. Patience is of the essence in this instance.

10. Talk to yourself – in front of a mirror

This chapter deals with a method of learning to speak French that is not common but which is effective.

Generally, talking to oneself is frowned upon or could be a sign of loneliness in elderly people. Neither is the case in this instance. Talking to yourself in French in front of a mirror will not get you a frown or be attributed to an early onset of senility, I can assure you. On the contrary, it will guarantee you effective results.

Here again, your brain is all vanity, all ego. While you attempt to pronounce a French word or sentence in front of a mirror, your brain will not only register the sounds you make much faster, but it will remember the images of your mouth articulating the words. And, I am very sorry to say that you'll become your own French Monkey.

Very much like a child making faces in front of a mirror, you'll be mouthing the words and storing sounds and images in your brain – to be retrieved later in front of an interlocutor.

As well as mouthing the words, you will automatically accompany the words or eventually sentences with helpful gestures that are understood the world over.

Here is the first example that comes to mind:

Say: "*Je*" pointing your index finger to your chest.

Say: "*Je mange*" pointing your index finger to your chest and chewing on an imaginary piece of food, etc.

Because the gestures and movements are exaggerated, your brain reacts and stores the hilarity of the scene – BUT at the same time it will never forget that "*je*" means "I or me" and that '*mange*' means 'chew or eat'.

Remember the toddler that you are when it comes to learning French. Don't be shy to make faces, to increase the gesticulating, to shout the words if you want – this is your French environment and yours alone.

Although not utilizing a mirror, this method is applied in many language immersion schools, because it works!

The second phase of this *talk to yourself* method is to talk to someone else – an imaginary French friend, or your pet dog or cat. Think of it as your French interlocutor – the person who will be (and is) listening to you while you try your best to get your message across.

Here's a little anecdote that should illustrate the importance of clear pronunciation. Even though the incident occurred between a Frenchman trying to speak English and an English woman trying to understand the man, the same would apply in reverse.

Years ago, my husband and I went to a club, sat down and decided to order some drinks during the intermission. The waitress came to the table to take the order. Pen poised, she listened to my husband order: "A foot bench"!

"Was that a foot bench?" she asked, visibly puzzled.

"Yes," my husband answered, "that is what I want; a foot bench."

Not wanting to argue, the dear girl went away after I had ordered an orange juice.

When she came back, she apologized profusely for not finding a "foot bench" on the premises.

My husband then turned to me and asked (in French) if I could tell the young woman what he wanted.

I nodded and looked up at the lady, saying, "My husband would like a "fruit punch"!"

There are very little differences between the two phrases: 'foot bench' and 'fruit punch'. However as subtle as they were, the young waitress didn't make the connection and could only understand one version of the two phrases.

What is interesting about this story is the omitted 'r' in 'fruit'. As a Frenchman, the husband had learned that rather than roll the 'r' as one does in French, you rather 'melt' (or incorporate) it with the next syllable –

which he did when pronouncing the word 'fruit' – and it became 'foot'. The next word 'punch' suffered another fate; instead of articulating the syllable 'un' he pronounced it as 'en', thus transforming the word 'punch' into 'bench'.

Therefore, and again, the correct pronunciation of the words is vital when learning a language. And while you're pronouncing each word that you learn in front of your mirror, you will soon notice when each of them is correctly articulated.

11. Let's go out!

Once you have mastered the art of pronouncing words and sentences in front of the mirror and in front of your imaginary French friend, I think it would be time for you to meet and greet your friend and perhaps go into 'explaining' who you are and what you do all day.

Whatever the purpose behind your learning French, you will inevitably come in contact with French-speaking people. In English a 'first impression' is very important in any given circumstance, and so it is in French. People in French-speaking countries have tendencies of 'judging' you by not only their first impression of you, but also by the manner in which you conduct yourself. A polite behavior is essential. Next comes the way you dress – if you wear the wrong clothes for the circumstances, you could be in trouble. Then there is food – what you eat and how you eat will set you apart as either a gentleman or a lady, or a peasant. 'Faux pas' is French for 'the wrong step' or putting your foot in your mouth!

Therefore, and to help you on your way of making a 'fantastic' first impression, I have put together lists of common phrases and items that you will use on a daily basis in a French environment – weather at your local French Club or during a trip to a French-speaking country. Remember, you are a toddler in a new environment. You're learning to:

- Greet people,
- Be polite,
- Dress appropriately,
- Eat and drink in public,
- Watch your manners,
- Enjoy yourself in this new society.

French Greetings

The only greeting words you need to remember are *bonjour* and *bonsoir*. Bonjour means hello, and is used throughout the day. Bonsoir, on the other hand, is only used in the evening. As for good morning – *'bon matin'* – it is wrong! And good afternoon – *'bonne après midi'* – is rarely used and only as goodbye, when you leave someone in the afternoon.

If you wanted to say good night to a member of your family or a loved one, you may use *bonne nuit*. However, when you leave a place of work, you <u>do not say</u> 'bonne nuit' to your co-workers, colleagues, or even friends you meet at the pub after work. 'Bonne nuit' is reserved for 'people close to you' – that's all.

Another word that is used frequently any time of the day or night – except with family or loved ones – is *'salut'*. It is a casual hello or hi.

Again the circumstances will dictate whether you say *'bonjour' or 'salut'* to someone. However, remember that in French society, a smile will not suffice to acknowledge or greet someone – you need to say the word to the person and even shake hands with him or her. Of course, you won't shake hands every time you meet the butcher in his shop, but you need to greet him. And if you know his name, by all means use it. You would then say, *"Bonjour, Monsieur Durant."*

The same goes in public places or transport, you would greet the bus driver with a casual *bonjour* and when you have been invited to a social gathering of any sort, you will need to go round the room and greet everyone individually. Shake hands (*serrer la main*) is usually the acceptable way to introduce your greeting, but occasionally a lady that you may know will extend a cheek towards you for you to give her a peck. Grandmothers, aunts, and cousins will do that.

French people are exceptionally demonstrative in their manners and behaviors. They will kiss you (on the cheeks), they will hug you, they'll take you by the hand to introduce you to someone else, and they will even bring you a tray of appetizers or snacks if they sense that you're too shy to take the first step toward the buffet. But, be sure to know that none of these gestures of friendship have any ulterior motive. For example; you've been invited to a party and the young, beautiful hostess takes you by the arm and leads you around the room, chats with you, gives you a peck on the cheek, and even takes the first steps on the dance floor with you; do not think for one minute that you're going to share her bed that night – because it is not going to happen!

Introduce yourself and others

When you want to introduce yourself to a person or to a group of people there are several phrases to remember.

Permettez-moi de me présenter – Let me introduce myself.

Je m'appelle Micheline – My name is Micheline.

Je suis Monsieur Durant – I am Mr. Durant.

Mon prénom est Pierre – My first name is Pierre.

Mon nom de famille est Durant – My family name (surname) is Durant.

Generally the introductions between two people are quite informal. Here are some examples:

Bonjour, Je m'appelle Micheline, et vous êtes? – Hi, my name is Micheline and you are?

Oh bonjour, moi c'est Pierre, Pierre Durant – Oh hi, I'm Pierre, Pierre Durant.

Enchantée de faire votre connaissance, Pierre, comment allez-vous? – Nice to meet you, Pierre, how are you?

Introducing others:

If Pierre and/or Micheline are in company of others, they will each introduce their friends or acquaintances this way:

Permettez-moi de vous présenter Monsieur Dubois, mon voisin – Let me introduce you to Mr. Dubois, my neighbor.

OR

Permets-moi de te présenter Sylvette, mon amie – Let me introduce you to Sylvette, my girlfriend.

OR

Et voici Monsieur et Madame Duval, des amis de ma famille – And here are Mr. and Mrs. Duval, friends of my family.

OR

When not directly facing the person, you may introduce his or her name this way:

Il s'appelle Jean. Je vais au collège avec lui – His name is Jean. I go to college with him.

OR

Elle s'appelle Marie. C'est une autre de mes voisines – Her name is Marie. It's another one of my neighbors.

Meeting people you want to know

When mingling among people at a party for example, once you have introduced yourself (as above) you may ask:

Comment vous appelez-vous? (Formal and/or plural) – What is (are) your name(s)?

Comment t'appelles-tu? (Informal) – What is your name?

The answer may be: 'Enchanté/enchantée' or 'Charmé/charmée'.

Next: Let's set up a date for your next meeting.

French Calendar

The French calendar – *le calendrier* – is similar to the English calendar. It is a good idea to familiarize yourself with the days of the week – *les jours de la semaine* – and with the months of the year – *les mois de l'année* – and with the time of day – *les heures de la journée* – to be able to set up a date and time for your next meeting.

Lundi – Monday.

Mardi – Tuesday.

Mercredi – Wednesday.

Jeudi – Thursday.

Vendredi – Friday.

Samedi – Saturday.

Dimanche – Sunday.

These are the days of the week. In written French, these nouns are not capitalized.

J'ai vu ce filme dimanche dernier – I saw that movie last Sunday.

Je commence le travail lundi matin – I start (the) work on Monday morning.

The above are singular events. In the case of multiple events, you can expect to hear the days used with a definite article in front of each.

*Je rencontre Suzanne **le** lundi* – I meet Suzanne on Monday(s).

*Je fais mes commissions **le** samedi* – I do my shopping on Saturday(s).

Janvier – January.

Février – February.

Mars – March.

Avril – April.

Mai – May.

Juin – June.

Juillet – July.

Août – August.

Septembre – September.

Octobre – October.

Novembre – November.

Décembre – December.

Note that the months of the year – *les mois de l'année* – are not capitalized either, except when starting a sentence.

Je le vois en octobre – I see him in October

Les quatre saisons de l'année commencent

– en décembre – *l'hiver*

   – en mars – *le printemps*

– en juin – *l'été*

– et en septembre – *l'automne.*

Printemps – spring.

Été – summer.

Automne – autumn/fall.

Hiver – winter.

Your next step in setting the date for your next meeting would be to know the time you would like to meet him or her.

Actually 'time' only translates one way in French, and that's 'temps'. When you ask a person "What *time* is it?" you will need to ask "quelle *heure* est-il?" – What hour is it?

To set up a meeting, you need to ask:

A quelle **heure** veux-tu aller au restaurant?

At what **time** do you want to go to the restaurant?

The answer would probably be:

A sept heure, je serai au restaurant – At seven o'clock, I will be at the restaurant.

Or

A sept heure du soir – At 7:00pm.

Here are some example of times and the way to phrase the statement or question.

Quelle heure est-il? – What time is it?

Il est trois heures – 3h00 – It's three o'clock.

Il est trois heures et demie / Il est trois heures trente – 3h30 – It's 3:30 am.

Il est cinq heures et quart / Il est cinq heures quinze – 5h15 – It's 5:15 am.

Il est trois heures moins le quart / It's quater to three / *Il est deux heures quarante-cinq* – 2h45 – It's 2:45 am.

Il est quatre heures dix – 4h10 – It's 4:10 am.

Il est sept heures moins dix / Il est six heures cinquante – 6h50 – It's 6:50 am.

Il est huit heures du matin – 8h00 – It's 8:00 am.

Il est quatre heures de l'après-midi / Il est seize heures – 16h00 – It's 4:00 pm.

Il est sept heures du soir / Il est dix-neuf heures – 19h00 – It's 7:00 pm.

Il est midi – 12h00 – It's noon.

Il est minuit – 0h00 – It's midnight.

Now that you've set up a date and time for your next meeting, let's see what you're going to wear.

Les Vêtements – the garments (or clothes)

But before we get dressed, let's take a shower!

We need:

Du savon – Soap.

Du shampoing – Shampoo.

Une éponge – Sponge

Une brosse à dents – Toothbrush.

De la pâte dentifrice – Toothpaste.

Un rasoir – Razor.

Crème à raser – Shaving cream.

Essuie-mains (hand cloth) ou serviettes de bain – (bath towels).

Okay, let's get dressed.

For a man:

Un caleçon – Underwear.

Des chaussettes – Socks.

Un tee-shirt – T-shirt.

Une chemise – Shirt.

Une cravate – Tie.

Des pantalons – Trousers.

Un costume – Suit.

Un smoking – Tuxedo.

Une ceinture – Belt.

Un pull (Sweater) gilet (Vest).

Une jaquette, un veston – Jacket.

Des chaussures – Shoes.

Un manteau – Coat.

Un imperméable – Raincoat.

Un chapeau – Hat.

Une paire de gants – A pair of gloves.

If your rendezvous is a casual one, you'll need a different set of clothes.

Un anorak – Anorak.

Un béret – Beret.

Une écharpe – Muffler.

Des moufles – Mitts.

Des bottes – Boots.

Des tennis – Running shoes, sneakers.

Un short – Shorts.

Une camisole – T-shirt, sweat shirt.

Costume de bain – Bathing suit.

Slip de bain – Swimming trunks.

For a woman:

Un slip – Panties.

Des collants ou des bas – Pantyhose or stockings.

Un soutien-gorge – A bra.

Une blouse ou un chemisier – A shirt.

Une jupe – A skirt.

Une robe – A dress.

Une jaquette – A jacket.

Des pantalons pour dames – Women's trousers.

Des chaussures à talons – High-heel shoes.

Des talons aiguilles – Stiletto heels.

Un manteaux – A coat.

Un cardigan – A sweater/cardigan.

Un chapeau – A hat.

Des sandales – Sandals.

Okay... What's missing?

Jewelry and accessories, of course

Pour madame:

Un collier – A necklace.

Un bracelet – A bracelet.

Des boucles d'oreilles – Earrings.

Une broche – A brooch.

Une bague – A ring.

Une bague de fiançailles – An engagement ring.

Un sac à main – A handbag.

Des gants – Gloves.

Un portable – Cell phone or mobile.

Un bâton de rouge à lèvres – Lipstick.

Un poudrier – A compact (powder).

Un peigne – A comb.

Pour monsieur:

Une épingle de cravate – A tie pin.

Des boutons de manchettes – Cufflinks.

Une montre – A watch.

Une chevalière – A signet ring.

Une alliance – A wedding ring.

Un portefeuille – A wallet.

Les clés de voiture – Car keys.

De l'argent – Some money.

De la monnaie – Some change.

Un mouchoir – a handkerchief.

Un parapluie – An umbrella.

Okay, now that Micheline and Pierre are ready, Pierre will take his car and pick up his date at her place.

La voiture – The car.

Une deux portes – A two-door.

Une quatre portes – A four-door.

Une automatique – Automatic.

Direction assistée – Assisted steering.

Sièges ajustables – Adjustable seating.

Quatre-quatre – Four-wheel drive.

Climatisée – Air-conditioned.

Chauffage – Heater.

Deux-chevaux – Two-horse power.

Six pistons – Six cylinders.

Le moteur – The motor.

Essuie-glaces – Windshield/windscreen wipers.

Les clignotants – The turning signals.

L'accélérateur – The gas pedal.

Les freins – The brakes.

Débrayer – Engage a gear.

Sièges arrières – Back seats.

Sièges avants – Front seats.

Le coffre – Trunk or boot.

Sous le capot – Under the hood (or bonnet).

Le rétroviseur – Rear-view mirror.

Les ailes – The fenders.

Le radiateur – The radiator.

L'essence – Gas or petrol.

L'huile à moteur – The motor oil.

Les amortisseurs – La suspension.

Arriving at Micheline's place – an apartment...

La porte d'entrée – Front door.

La sonnette – Doorbell.

Ouvrir et fermer la porte – Open and close the door.

Le corridor – Corridor.

Le couloir – The hallway.

La salle à manger – The dining room.

La table de salle à manger – The dining room table.

Les chaises – The dining room chairs.

Le buffet – The sideboard.

Le vaisselier – The cupboard for dishes (exclusively in France).

La cuisine – The Kitchen.

Le réchaud, la cuisinière – The stove, cooker.

Le réfrigérateur ou la glacière ou frigo – The fridge.

Les armoires – The cupboards, closets.

Le comptoir – The counter.

Les appareils ménagers – The kitchen appliances.

La table de cuisine – The kitchen table.

Le salon – The living (or lounge) room.

Le divan – The sofa.

Les fauteuils – The chairs.

Les lampes – The table or floor lamps.

La table de salon – The coffee table.

Les tapis – The throw-rugs.

Le plancher – The floor (of a room i.e. hardwood floor).

Les peintures – The paintings.

Des ornements – The ornaments.

La chambre à coucher – The bedroom.

Le lit – The bed.

La table de nuit – The night table.

La garde-robe – The wardrobe.

Le dressoir – The dresser.

La salle de bain – The bathroom.

La baignoire – The bathtub.

La toilette – The toilet.

L'évier – The sink.

Et voilà, nous partons au restaurant….And there we go to the restaurant….

Un restaurant français – A French restaurant.

The maitre d' (le maitre d'hôtel) will meet Pierre and Micheline as they come in the restaurant, greet them and probably ask: *"Bonsoir, monsieur, madame. Une table pour deux?"* – Good evening, sir, ma'am. A table for two?

Upon Pierre saying, *"Oui, s'il vous plait,"* the maitre d' will usher them to their table and hand them a menu saying, *"Votre serveur (or serveuse) viendra prendre la commande dans un instant."* – Your waiter (or waitress) will come and take your order in a moment.

On an average restaurant's menu you will find five courses.

Les hors d'œuvres – Small appetizers.

Les plats d'entrée ou les soupes – Appetizers or soups.

Les plats consistants (or principal) – Main courses.

Les viandes, les poissons, volailles – meats, fish, poultry.

Les fromages – Cheeses.

Les déserts et les fruits – Desserts and fruit.

Les hors d'œuvres are generally small pastries filled with some delicacies, such as prawns (crevettes), clams (palourdes), crab (crabe) or cold cuts (viandes froides) in summer. These are bite-size and could be ordered for the table rather than the individual.

Les plats d'entrée may consist of the following:

Filet de sole – filet of sole.

Truite au beurre – trout in butter sauce.

Salade d'endives – Endive salad.

Crevettes à l'ail – Garlic shrimps (or prawns).

Note: in many French restaurants, you'll find seafood and fish listed as an appetizer on the menu. If you see fish as a main course, you could expect that it's a house specialty or something the chef prepares once in a while.

As for the soups, you have a great variety of soups to choose from, but mostly served in fall and winter, unless you find 'gazpacho' – a cold Spanish soup listed on the menu.

Les plats de consistances are generally comprised of meat, poultry, vegetables, potatoes, pastas, and some marinades or sauces.

Here is a list of meat, fish and poultry you might want to remember:

Veau – Veal.

Côtelettes de veau – Veal chops.

Bœuf – Beef.

Bifteck – Beefsteak.

Rôti de bœuf – Roast beef.

Au bleu – Rare.

Bien cuit – Well done.

Porc – Pork.

Côtes ou côtelettes de porc – Pork chops.

Rôti de porc – Porc roast.

Pieds de porc – Pigs feet.

Un jambon – A ham.

Agneau et mouton – Lamb and mutton.

Un gigot d'agneau (ou mouton) – Leg of lamb (or mutton).

Une tranche de mouton – A slice of mutton.

Lapin – Rabbit.

Escargots – Escargots (snails).

Des moules – Mussels.

Huîtres – Oysters.

Homards – Lobsters.

Ecrevisses – Crayfish.

Les poissons – Fish.

La sole – Sole.

Le cabillot – Halibut.

La truite – Trout.

Le saumon – Salmon.

(The fish you can buy or choose in restaurants are usually those available in the region and differ from country to country.)

Poulets – Chicken

Le blanc de poulet – Chicken breast.

Le cou – Neck.

Les cuisses – Thighs.

Les ailes – Wings.

Les pattes – Chicken feet (or legs).

Dindes ou dindons – Turkeys.

Une cuisse de dinde – Turkey thigh.

Un blanc de dinde – White meat.

Les sauces – Sauces

Vinaigrette – Oil and vinegar.

Mayonnaise – Mayonnaise.

Béarnaise – Béarnaise.

Au fromage – Cheese sauce.

Sauce blanche – White sauce.

Aioli or *à l'ail* – Garlic dressing.

Jus de viande – Broth.

As for vegetables..., here they are:

Une tomate – A tomato.

Une laitue – A head of lettuce.

Un oignon – An onion.

De l'ail – Some garlic.

Un artichaut – An artichoke.

Une asperge – An asparagus spear.

Une aubergine – An eggplant.

Une carotte – A carrot.

Une branche de céleri – A celery stick.

Un champignon – A mushroom.

Un chou-fleur – A cauliflower.

Un concombre – A cucumber.

Des épinards – Some spinach.

Un haricot vert – A green bean.

Des haricots blancs – Some white beans.

Des lentilles – Some lentils.

Des petits pois – Some peas.

Un poivron (vert, rouge, jaune) – A green, red, yellow pepper (or capsicum).

Du maïs – Corn or corn on a cob (not frequent in France).

Un brocoli – A head of broccoli.

Des patates douces – Some sweet potatoes.

Une pomme de terre – A potato.

Un radis – A radish.

Les cornichons – Dill pickles.

Les pâtes – Pastas.

Des spaghettis – Spaghettis.

Des vermicelles – Vermicelli.

Des raviolis – Raviolis.

Des lasagnes – Lasagnes.

Petits plats – The side dishes (appetizers generally).

Amuse-gueules – Fun bites.

Pommes frites – French fries, chips.

Du riz – Some rice.

Du riz sauvage – Some wild rice.

Next come the cheeses (Les fromages)

French people love their cheeses. Each region has one or more distinctive cheeses. There are literally hundreds of different cheeses in France. But here are some of the better known ones.

Le camembert – Camembert.

Le roquefort – Rockford.

Le brie – Brie.

Le chester – Cheddar.

L'édam – Edam.

Le gouda – Gouda.

L'emmental – Swiss cheese.

Le fromage blanc – Cream cheese – cream of cheese.

Les desserts:

La crème glacée – Ice cream.

Vanille – Vanilla.

Chocolat – Chocolate.

Fraise – Strawberry.

Framboises – Raspberries.

Amandes – Almonds.

Caramel – Butterscotch.

Crème brûlée – Custard with hot, brown sugar.

Mousse au chocolat – Chocolat mousse.

Crêpes Suzette – Crepes (Suzette).

Crêpes Flambées – Searing Crepes.

Bombe Alaska – Bomb Alaska.

Une meringue – Meringue.

Profiteroles – Custard-filled pastries.

Crème caramel – Flan.

Tartes – Pies.

Aux fraises – Strawberry pie.

Aux myrtilles – Blueberry pie.

Aux pommes – Apple pie.

Aux prunes – Plum pie.

Au fromage – Cheese pie (cake).

Les gâteaux – Cakes.

Les gâteaux de Savoie – Savoy cakes.

Les gâteaux au chocolat – Chocolate cakes.

Crème fraîche – Whipping cream.

And staple foods:

La farine – Flour.

Les croissants – Croissants.

La confiture – Preserves or jam.

Le pain – Bread.

La baguette – French baguette.

Un pistolet – Bun.

Un petit pain – Roll.

Un pain blanc – White bread.

Un pain gris – Brown bread.

Du café – Coffee.

Café au lait – Coffee with milk.

Café crème – Coffee with cream.

Biscuits – Cookies, biscuits.

Le yaourt – Yogurt.

Le lait – Milk.

Le beurre – Butter.

Huile d'olive – Olive oil.

Sel – Salt.

Poivre – Pepper.

Thym – Thyme.

Laurier – Bay leaves.

Next come the fruits – Fruits

Une orange – Orange.

Un pamplemousse – Grapefruit.

Un abricot – Apricot.

Une poire – Pear.

Une pomme – Apple.

Une prune – Plum.

Un ananas – Pineapple.

Une banane – Banana.

Des cerises – Cherries.

Un citron – Lemon.

Un citron vert – Lime.

Des mûres – Blackberries.

Des myrtilles – Blueberries.

Une pastèque – Watermelon.

Un melon – A melon.

Une citrouille – Pumpkin.

Des fruits de passion – Passion fruit.

Une pêche – Peach.

Des nectarines – Nectarines.

Raisins verts – Green grapes.

Les vins et les boissons

Un vin rouge – Red wine.

Un Bordeaux – A Bordeaux.

Un Beaujolais – A Beaujolais.

Un Cabernet Sauvignon – Cabernet Sauvignon.

Un Bourgogne – Burgundy wine.

Un vin blanc – White wine.

Blanc sec – Dry white wine.

Blanc fumé – 'Smoked' wine.

Un vin du Rhône – A wine from the Rhone region.

Un champagne – Champaign.

Brut – Brut.

Sec – Dry.

Eau minérale – Mineral water.

Boissons sans alcool – Non-alcoholic drinks.

Coca Cola – Coke.

Thé – Tea.

Bière – Beer.

Une liqueur – Liqueur.

Eau de vie – Specialty of France (Water of life).

Une goutte – A drop of liqueur (schnapps).

Un cognac – A cognac.

Un pousse-café – After dinner drink.

Now that Micheline and Pierre have eaten a scrumptious dinner, let's leave them and look at what their day will consist of during the week....

The routine – La routine

Le réveil – Wake up or waking up.

Le réveil – The alarm clock

La sonnette d'alarme – The alarm bell. (For emergency)

Sortir du lit – To get out of bed.

Se brosser les dents – To brush one's teeth.

Prendre une douche – To take a shower.

S'habiller – To get dressed.

Prendre un petit déjeuner – To eat breakfast.

Un café – A coffee.

Un croissant à la confiture – A croissant with jam.

Un jus d'orange – An orange juice.

Une omelette – An omelette.

Des œufs sur le plat – Eggs – sunny side up (or fried).

Du pain grillé – Toasts.

Des œufs brouillés – Scrambled eggs.

Du lard – Some bacon.

Un pain sucré – Sweet bread.

Partir au travail – Go to work.

Le métro – The underground.

Le bus – The bus.

Le train – The train.

La voiture – The car.

L'heure de pointe – The rush hour (going to work).

Arriver au bureau – To get to the office.

S'asseoir à son bureau – To take a seat at one's desk.

Les dossiers – The files and folders.

L'ordinateur – The computer.

Les courriels – The emails.

Le téléphone – Phone.

Le patron ou la patronne – The boss (he or she).

Les secrétaires – The secretaries.

Les clients – The clients.

Les vendeurs, les vendeuses – The sales persons (he or she).

Les marchants – The merchants or vendors.

Le banquier – The banker.

Le plombier – The plumber.

L'électricien – The electrician.

Le charpentier – The carpenter.

Le postier – The mail carrier, the postman.

Le gérant, la gérante – The manager (he or she).

Le directeur, la directrice – The director (he or she) (CEO).

Le (ou la) comptable – The accountant.

Le manœuvre – The labourer.

Le camionneur – The truck driver.

Le conducteur – The bus or train driver.

Un taxi – A cab or taxi.

Un chauffeur – A taxi or car driver.

Aller déjeuner – To go for lunch.

Au café du coin – At the corner deli or coffee shop.

Au restau – At the restaurant.

Dans le quartier – In the neighborhood.

Un pique-nique – A picnic.

Un sandwich – A sandwich.

Un bol de soupe – A bowl of soup.

Un pain beurré – A buttered bread.

Un petit fromage – Some cheese.

Un fruit – A fruit.

Reprendre le boulot – Go back to work.

Rentrer chez soi ou à la maison – Go home.

Aller chercher les enfants à l'école – Pick-up the children at school.

Un goûter – A snack (mostly for kids).

Jouer dans le jardin – To play in the garden (or backyard).

Faire les devoirs – To do one's homework.

Faire (préparer) le dîner – To prepare dinner.

Mettre la table – To set the table.

Manger à sa faim – Eat to one's appetite.

Débarrasser la table – Clear the table.

Faire la vaisselle – Do (wash) the dishes.

Regarder la télé – Watch TV.

Aller se coucher ou aller dormir – Go to bed or go to sleep.

I believe it is important to mention once again that, in all situations, French people will try to be as polite as possible. And if the opportunity presents itself for you to travel to France, it would be essential for you to remember that being polite will open you many doors. Same as you do with your children at home; perhaps you should endeavour to exercise French politeness wherever and whenever possible.

Here are some of the phrases:

S'il vous plaît – If you please or please (plural or formal).

S'il te plait – Please (familiar).

Veuillez m'excuser – Please, excuse me.

Merci ou merci beaucoup – Thank you or thank you very much.

De rien – You're welcome (it's nothing).

Pas de quoi – Don't mention it.

Je vous en prie – It was my pleasure.

Pardonnez-moi – Pardon me.

Pardonne-moi, que disais-tu? – I beg your pardon, what did you say?

Excusez-moi – Excuse me (formal).

Excusez-moi de vous déranger – Sorry to bother you (formal).

Je suis désolé(e) – I'm sorry.

Inevitably, when visiting another country, you will be asked about the weather at home. The question that will be asked most often will be:

Quel temps fait-il chez vous? – What's the weather like at your place?

The answer generally starts the same way for almost all weather conditions:

Il fait froid / chaud dans notre pays – It's cold / warm (hot) in our country.

En hiver il fait froid – In winter it is cold.

Il y a du vent – It's windy.

Il neige – It snows.

Il pleut – It rains.

Il y a du verglas – There is some ice (on the roads).

Il y a du brouillard – It's foggy.

Le temps est glacial – The weather is ice-cold.

Le vent vient du nord – The wind comes from the north.

Il y a de gros nuages – There are some big clouds.

En été il fait chaud – In summer it is hot.

Il fait humide – It is humid.

Il y a des orages – There are some storms.

Le vent est frais – The wind is cool.

Le ciel est bleu – The sky is blue.

Il fait beau – The weather is beautiful.

Il n'y a pas de vent – There is no wind.

Il grêle – It's hailing.

Il y a du soleil – It's sunny.

French Numbers

The last of the vocabulary listings that I'd like you to remember is perhaps the easiest to remember.

Zéro – zero (0).

Un, une – one (1).

Deux – two (2).

Trois – three (3).

Quatre – four (4).

Cinq – five (5).

Six – six (6).

Sept – seven (7).

Huit – eight (8).

Neuf – nine (9).

Dix – ten (10).

Onze – eleven (11).

Douze – twelve (12).

Treize – thirteen (13).

Quatorze – fourteen (14).

Quinze – fifteen (15).

Seize – sixteen (16).

Dix-sept – seventeen (17).

Dix-huit – eighteen (18).

Dix-neuf – nineteen (19).

Vingt – twenty (20).

Vingt-et-un – twenty-one (21).

Trente – thirty (30).

Quarante – forty (40).

Cinquante – fifty (50).

Soixante – sixty (60).

Soixante-dix ou septante – seventy (70).

Quatre-vingt ou octante – eighty (80).

Quatre-vingt-dix ou nonante – ninety (90).

Cent – hundred (100)

The only complication you may find with these numbers is their pronunciation. Their pronunciation changes whether they precede a word starting with a vowel or a consonant.

For example:

Cinq – Q is audible.

Cinq francs – Q is audible (or silent).

Cinq enfants – Q is audible.

Cinq centimes – Q is audible (or silent depending on the regional prononciation).

Huit – is pronounced 'weet' – T is audible.

Huit cylindres (eight cylinders) – T is silent.

The last letter of the numbers *cinq, six, huit* and *dix*, when preceding a consonant, is often silent.

12. Repeating what you learn – *en famille*

Throughout this book I have listed an extensive current vocabulary, which is not for you to use as a dictionary or word reference pages.

All the words listed should be repeated in front of a mirror until you are satisfied that your pronunciation is correct.

You could try to include family members into this exercise. Let's see what a French family consists of:

Le père – The father.

Papa – Dad or Daddy.

Mon père et son papa sont allés à la pêche – My father and his dad went fishing.

La mère – The mother.

Maman – Mom or Mommy.

Maman fait la cuisine avec sa mère – Mom is cooking with her mother.

Le frère – The brother.

La sœur – The sister.

J'ai trois frères et deux sœurs – I have three brothers and two sisters.

Le cousin – The cousin (masculine).

La cousine – The cousin (feminine).

La tante – The aunt.

L'oncle – The uncle.

Ma tante et mon oncle vivent en France – My aunt and uncle live in France.

Le neveu – The nephew.

La nièce – The niece.

Mon neveu est plus âgé que ma nièce – My nephew is older than my niece.

Les parents – The parents.

Les grands-parents – The grand parents.

Ses parents et mes grands-parents se connaissent depuis longtemps – Her/his parents and my grandparents know each other for a long time.

Le grand-père – The grandfather.

Pépé or Papy (or Papi) – Granddad.

Les enfants aiment leur bon-papa – The children love their granddad.

La grand-mère – The grandmother.

Mémé or Mamie – Grandma.

Ma grand-mère n'est pas très âgée – My grandmother is not very old.

Le parrain – The godfather.

La marraine – The godmother.

Son parrain est fortuné – His/her godfather is wealthy.

La belle-mère – The mother-in-law.

Le beau-père – The father-in-law.

Every 'in-law' is translated by 'beau' or 'belle' as in 'belle-sœur' or 'beau-frère'.

Members of your family would probably enjoy listening to you speak French, because, by this time, you should be able to articulate words properly and construct sentences on your own.

Conclusion

There are many ways to learn a language, but there are only two ways to learn to **speak** a language. To learn to speak French you could go to a French-speaking country, spend several months among French people while being immersed in their culture and customs, or you could bring the French culture, customs and environment to you.

However, the **easiest** and most **effective** way to learn to speak any language is not only to immerse yourself in the language's environment but to understand that **your brain is only a toddler** when it comes to learning to speak a different language from your own.

Throughout the preceding pages, we have introduced you to a process by which you **do not teach** yourself to speak French, but you **train your brain** to remember, memorize and imitate French sounds – the sounds each word makes. Moreover, this self-immersion system is designed to encourage your brain to register subconsciously the phrases, sentences, and expressions it hears as often as possible.

By repeating the words you hear, the sentences you construct, using the construction blocks we have given you, you are training the toddler in you to register and understand what is said, or what you say.

I encourage you to enunciate each word you learn in front of a mirror, because your brain not only registers sounds but images. When you pronounce a French consonant properly, the image of your mouth and facial expression remains in the recesses of your brain to be retrieved when teased to do so, or when needed.

You could take courses to learn to write French, but I urge you to consider a self-training program, such as the one described and used in this book to teach yourself to speak French.

French is an easy language to learn because it is an organized language. There are very few surprises waiting for you, very few idioms to remember, and very few exceptions to the rules. What's more, when you use a dictionary or a word reference dictionary, they will help you in constructing phrases and sentences without much hesitation.

Other great beginner books on Amazon that can teach you about the basics of the French Language are these 2 great cheapies below. I think these books are a great buy for the beginner regarding the quality of knowledge, structure of learning and basic fundamentals of the language.

French. Practice for Perfection by Antoine Pelletier

French Words, Phrases and Sentences. 1000+ by Michel Durand